THE NIGHT'S SWEET EMBRACE

Other Works by Bethany Davis:

The Moon and Stars of the Dark Night Sky:
The Moon and Stars of the Dark Night Sky (Book I)
The Chasm of Mist (Book II)

THE NIGHT'S SWEET EMBRACE

POEMS OF THE MEETINGS AND PARTINGS
OF CELESTE AND HER SOPHIA

THE MOON AND STARS OF THE DARK NIGHT SKY
BOOK III

BETHANY DAVIS

Caer Illandria Publishing
Broomfield, CO

Copyright © 2019 by Bethany Davis. All rights reserved.

"I Turn," "The Night Devours You," "All," "Only Love," and "Tangible and Clear" previously published in The Moon and Stars of the Dark Night Sky, copyright © 2015

"Safe at Home Secure," "Heart's Delight," "The Place I Long," and "The Dark Night Sky" previously published in The Chasm of Mist, copyright © 2017

All poems dated with original copyright, © 2011-2019

"Consider the Vastness" references the line, "Out here in the perimeter there are no stars." This line is from poetry by Jim Morrison, contained in "The WASP (Texas Radio and the Big Beat)," a song released on the album L.A. Woman, April 19, 1971

"As We Wind" quotes the line "As we wind on down the road," and references the piper in the lines, "Then the piper will lead us to reason" and "The piper is calling you to join him." All three lines are from Stairway to Heaven by Jimmy Page and Robert Plant, released on the album Led Zeppelin IV, November 8, 1971

For information please address:

Caer Illandria Enterprises
P.O. Box 7557
Broomfield, CO 80021

books@caerillandria.com
www.caerillandria.com

Printed in the United States of America

First Edition

ISBN-10: 0-9986200-2-5
ISBN-13: 978-0-9986200-2-2

For my Sophia, my Dark Night Sky, my Muse, my Song. I love you so very much. At last we are in one place, at last the meetings and partings are done. Thank you for never giving up on me, on us. I know the journey was hard. But at last I am in your arms each time we sleep, your moon and stars, at so long last, are in Night's Sweet Embrace.

CONTENTS

I TURN	1
THE NIGHT DEVOURS YOU	3
ALL	7
ONLY LOVE	9
TANGIBLE AND CLEAR	11
SAFE AT HOME SECURE	13
HEART'S DELIGHT	15
HOLD ME, LOVE	17
THE DARK NIGHT SKY	19
THE PLACE I LONG	21
BRING THE MOON TO LIGHT	23
HAPPY AS I CAN BE	25
YOUR SWEET ARMS	27
ALICE, LOST IN HER LOVER'S ARMS	29
A MILLION STARS	31
I HATE TO LEAVE	33
AS WE WIND	35
MY HATES AND MY LOVES	39
BLUSHING GIRL	41
HOW DO YOU HOLD THE RAGING WIND	43
ABOVE ALL ELSE	45
RETURNING	47
THE SUN ON MORNING DEW	49
ON RUSHING AND LAZINESS	51
THE TWILIT LANDS	53
BY DAWN'S GOLDEN LIGHT	55
YOUR EMBRACE	57
IN FROM THE COLD	59
IN THE MORNING LIGHT	61
MEMORIES STOLEN FROM TIME	63
THAT BOOK THAT HAS NEVER BEEN WRITTEN	65
A RING AROUND THE MOON, MY LOVE	69
SIMPLE WORDS	71
BY THE GATE	73
DOUBTING PLANES	75
THE MOMENT OF WAKING	77
IT'S WORTH IT	79
THE MOON ON MY RIGHT	81

DANCING THROUGH THOUGHTS AND MEMORIES	83
MY LOVER SLEEPS	85
BITTER WATER	87
A WORLD APART	89
ETERNAL LOVE	91
TRAVEL WORN	93
RISING IN THE EERIE SKY	95
A SLIVER MOON	97
WHAT ARE THE STARS?	99
THE MILES SPEED BY	101
SOUTHWARD BOUND	103
THE MYRIAD MISSING MIST	105
NEON CODE	107
LIKE FALLING LEAVES	111
SOON	115
EACH DAY	117
PASSING TIME	119
SO HOW LONG CAN?	121
LIQUID GOLD	123
THOSE DEPTHS THAT RISE SO HIGH	124
THIS JOURNEY TO THE NORTH	126
I MISSED YOU SO	129
THE GENTLE SPEED OF BREATH	133
THERE IS MY ONLY HOME	135
OUR LIVES ENTWINED	137
CONSIDER THE VASTNESS	139

Your memory feels like home to me. So whenever my mind wanders, it always finds its way back to you.
— Ranata Suzuki

I Turn

Celeste, Selene, Luna.
Moonlight on water, wind across the waves,
Night's sweet embrace.
I rise from the water,
Dripping, flowing, down my naked back.
Cold wind, I shiver, exposed but free.
Moonlight on water drops, my skin pale.
Peaceful night, silent, alone.
Not alone.
Eyes on me.
I turn.

~May 2, 2011

Bethany Davis

The Night Devours You

Inspired by the words of an amazing girl,
My Sophia, including some of hers

Look to the sky,
Feel the Night's presence.
Night's embrace,
The arms of Darkness hold you.
The Night envelops you,
It is hungry,
The Night devours you.
Lost in it.

As you are consumed,
You consume.
As the night devours you,
You devour.
Consumed becomes consumer,
Devouring yourself, one with yourself.
The Night and you are one.

Standing in the Void of Space,
Alone,
But not alone.
You are Night,
You are God Herself,
Nuit, full of stars.
Complete in yourself,
Unneeding,
Eternally satisfied.

Bethany Davis

The Mirror before you,
Yourself, looking at yourself,
In the Dark Mirror,
The curve of space.
Complete and alone,
Not alone.
Other.
Self.

You step towards.
She steps towards.
Night sees Night,
Embrace,
Passion.
She is you.
You are Night.
She is Night.
One.

Love, ecstasy.
Coupling, self with self.
Sex.
Orgasm.
Power.
Consumed.
Lost.

The Night's Sweet Embrace

Worlds spin away,
Creation begins.
Light out of Darkness.
Let there be light.
Shaking from passion.
Vibrations between atoms.
Night, proton.
Electron and neutron,
Twins, Divine Twins.
Big Bang, Big Orgasm.
Stars, the substance of stars.
Every man and woman is a star.

When it is dark enough, you can see the stars.

~April 19, 2011

Bethany Davis

All

Across the stars of a million years,
And all that's come and gone,
I walk with you, my heart, my soul,
And all I long to be.

You are my hopes, you are my dreams,
My lover through eternity,
I walk with you, my heart, my soul,
And all I hope to be.

If we're together or we're apart,
You're always here with me,
I walk with you, my heart, my soul,
And all I want to be.

The stars and moon in the midnight sky,
Me in your loving arms,
I walk with you, my heart, my soul,
And all I need to be.

~February 13, 2015

Bethany Davis

Only Love

Longing I feel in my very soul,
For my only love,
The distance that stands in the way,
Is hard, so hard to bear,
But in my heart and in my soul,
You're ever here with me,
And the distance is but for a time,
And in your arms I'll be,
I miss you love, my only love,
I long for your embrace,
And in your arms I will soon rest,
The waiting finally done,
You are my soul, you are my heart,
My one and only love,
My tomcat, sexy wildcat,
My only delight,
And so I wait for that day to come,
When I do come to you,
And in your arms I will soon rest,
The waiting finally done.

~February 15, 2015

Bethany Davis

Tangible and Clear

Mists condense, now solid form,
Now I have known your touch,
Each little bit, of my fair skin,
Longs for your embrace,
What once was mist, and hope of hope,
I've tasted and I've felt,
And know much more, than passing mist,
Held tight in loving arms,
And mist and shadow, that used to dance,
Now tangible and clear,
No more I long, for what I've never known,
For now I know your touch,
And flights of fancy, now manifest,
Memory is more than thought,
My body longs, for what it's felt,
The mist that then took form,
My solid love, with my own hands,
I held and touched and stroked,
You are not mist, or shadowed hope,
Your darkness I have felt,
And moon and stars, in dark night sky,
Held finally in your arms,
Two wolves we ran, two ravens flew,
Two snakes that twisted round,
Mists condense, and shadows form,
And we are who we are,
No longer thought, of what might be,
The memory of your touch,
Mists condense, and shadows form,
And we are who we are,
And tangible, I've held my love,
And will forevermore.

~March 31, 2015

Bethany Davis

The Night's Sweet Embrace

Safe at Home Secure

In your arms, I long to be, each breath a breath that's shared,
Skin on skin in cool night air, each move a sweet caress,
Drifting in and out of sleep, but knowing you're right there,
Safe we are with our own true loves, safe at home secure.

Hold me, love, as I lie awake, hold me as I sleep,
Breathe my breath and let me breathe, the air that is your breath,
Touch me love and feel my skin, caress my soft warm skin,
Safe we are with our own true loves, safe at home secure.

When I move and walk and pace, it's never very far,
And soon I return to your sweet arms, that hold me in the dark,
Nowhere else I long to be, but only with my love,
Safe we are with our own true loves, safe at home secure.

~April 13, 2015

Bethany Davis

Heart's Delight

You are my love,
My heart's delight,
You make my blood run hot.

I long for you,
Both day and night,
I long for your sweet embrace.

The time has been,
The time will come,
When I sleep there in your arms.

And for that day,
I yearn and pray,
And can't wait until it comes.

~April 27, 2015

Bethany Davis

Hold Me, Love

With your arm around me, love,
I feel so safe and warm,
You hold me tight, keep out the light,
That would mean we have to wake,
Each moment there I smile in bliss,
And want it not to end,
There in a dream or like a dream,
Your arms around me still,
Hold me, love, beneath the moon,
And in the morning light,
Hold me, love, through all of time,
No matter where we go,
There is one home that I have known,
One home I'll ever know,
And that is in your loving arms, my love,
Where I feel all safe and warm.

~April 30, 2015

Bethany Davis

The Dark Night Sky

The dark night sky,
Where I long to be,
Where my stars shine,
And my moon is full,
Of her I think,
In noon day sun,
Of her I think,
In the darkest nights,
The sky may rain,
And the sky may storm,
Snow might fall,
Or great big hail,
But in her arms,
I always shine,
The moon and stars,
Of the dark night sky.

~July 8, 2015

Bethany Davis

The Place I Long

The day draws near, my heart, my love,
When in your arms I'll be once more,
And all the waiting and all the pain,
Is worth this soon return.

And if I come to where you are,
Or if you come to me,
There is one place I want to be,
And it's both here and there.

The place I long and wish to be,
The place to which I return,
That place is not far away,
Nor is it ever near.

For where I long and wish to be,
The centre of my world,
Is in your strong and loving arms,
That's where I soon will be.

~July 30, 2015

Bethany Davis

Bring the Moon to Light

The sky so dark and full of stars,
Which holds the moon so close,
Caressing her skin each long night,
As she explores the fair night sky,
And every touch is silver light,
And every movement divine,
The night sky's arms that hold her tight,
Each long and stormy night.

The sky so dark and full of stars,
Which holds the moon so close,
And finds those places none can see,
To make her shine her light,
Moving hands each long night,
That explore her body fair,
The night sky's arms that hold her tight,
Each long and stormy night.

The sky so dark and full of stars,
Which holds the moon so tight,
Wandering hand and tongues and teeth,
That bring the moon delight,
And with each lick her light does grow,
From crescent to full light,
The night sky's arms that hold her tight,
Each long and stormy night.

Bethany Davis

The sky so dark and full of stars,
Which holds the moon so tight,
A tongue of fire in fading light,
That is the moon's delight,
Each stroke of tongue on skin so fair,
She brings the moon to light,
The night sky's arms that hold her tight,
Each long and stormy night.

The sky so dark and full of stars,
Which holds the moon so tight,
The moon all spent and fading now,
In the peace of afterglow,
And in her arms she's safe, content,
Fading now to dark,
The night sky's arms that hold her tight,
Each long and stormy night.

The sky so dark and full of stars,
Which holds the moon so tight,
There she hides, the dark new moon,
There in her lover's arms,
Memories of each long touch,
And dreams of each stroking tongue,
The night sky's arms that hold her tight,
Each long and stormy night.

~September 6, 2015

Happy as I Can Be

When I'm in my baby's arms,
I'm happy as I can be,
No worries there, no fear or cares,
And nothing can hurt me there.

I miss your touch, I miss your skin,
I miss your sweet, sweet kiss,
I miss your arms around me firm,
And you pressed against me so.

You held me, love, you will again,
And soon that day will come,
Where it's not upon a visit scarce,
But each and every day.

I'll come to you in morning light,
And come to you at night,
You'll come to me each and every day,
We'll lie in bed as one.

The warmth of you against my skin,
My touch upon your skin,
Each moment stretching on and on,
Each moment all there is.

For when I'm in my baby's arms,
I'm happy as I can be,
No worries there, no fear or cares,
And nothing can hurt me there.

~September 26, 2015

Bethany Davis

Your Sweet Arms

I miss you, love, when I sleep,
I miss you when I wake,
I miss you when I'm out at work,
I miss you when I'm home,
I miss you so, each and every day,
I miss you with all of me,
But soon I'll be in your sweet arms,
Soon I'll come to you.

I long for you in morning light,
I long for you at night,
I long for you when we talk,
I long when we're apart,
I long more each long day,
I long more as time goes by,
But soon I'll be in your sweet arms,
Soon I'll come to you.

I pine for you with each long breath,
I pine for you so much,
I pine for you with all my soul.
I pine for you so bad,
I pine for you when I have to wait,
I pine for you some more,
But soon I'll be in your sweet arms,
Soon I'll come to you.

I lust for you when I'm awake,
I lust for you in sleep,
I lust for you in bright sunlight,
I lust for you at night,
I lust for you like nothing else,
I lust for you alone,
But soon I'll be in your sweet arms,
Soon I'll come to you.

~October 15, 2015

Bethany Davis

Alice, Lost in Her Lover's Arms

On I wander,
Round and round,
Lost and much content,
Through the hills,
And valleys low,
And all around that place,
A wonderland,
I have found,
And ever love to roam,
A wonderland,
I might consume,
Or only touch and feel,
There is no place,
I'd rather be,
Nor way that I might be,
Lost among the rolling hills,
And valleys sweet and strong,
A wonderland,
Like none I've found,
Nor ever will again,
And as I roam,
And taste and feel,
And as I wander on,
This wonderland,
Is all I want,
To ever pine and dream,
And all the days,
And sweet hot nights,
And all times in between,
I may be Alice,
Lost and found,
In my dear lover's arms.

~October 10, 2015

Bethany Davis

A Million Stars

A million stars and a million more,
As far as the eye can see,
Light the night like my love for you,
Across the many years,
Flashing bright and sparkling on,
Like each though for you,
All the stars in all the sky,
Each and every light,
Don't shine at even half the shine,
Of how you make me yearn,
Each day I wait for your strong arms,
Each night I wait and long,
Feels like the time the stars do wait,
For the final end of time,
But though it's long and though I pine,
My hope it rises up,
And in my heart and in my soul,
I know we'll reach that time,
When the shining moon and all the stars,
Are held by the dark, dark, night.

~October 25, 2015

Bethany Davis

I Hate to Leave

I hate to leave,
My only love,
If only for a time,
I love to come,
To her strong arms,
Whenever the time does come,
It is the sweetest,
Sweetest balm,
Each time I come home,
But when I leave,
I always grieve,
Though I will come again,
Down the hole,
I'm want to go,
And through the looking glass,
To wander on,
Like Alice did,
It's strange apart from you,
I will return,
My only love,
I always come back to you,

Bethany Davis

For you are home,
My only home,
The place I do belong,
Whisper, love,
Into my ear,
And tell me of our love,
Your breath,
Your voice,
Your loving touch,
Is all I want or need,
This Alice lost,
Your own missing,
Always will come home,
Soon my love I'll come again,
Soon to your loving arms,
Lost I am,
And lost I be,
Until I come again,
Found I am,
And found I be,
In your arms forevermore.

~November 22, 2015

As We Wind

"And as we wind,
"on down the road,"
The words echo,
And they call,
Like the piper's,
Eternal call,
Time that echoes,
Years that crawl,
Do you remember,
I hear me say,
When the stars,
Came round before,
Eons gone and eons came,
You and me,
Are back again,
Do you remember,
Do you recall,
How I always,
Come back to you,
My one and only,
Through all of time,
Where white knights,
And red red queens,
Are talking backwards,
Like the hands of time,
The roads we wind down,
The paths we take,
That always lead back,
To your arms again,

Bethany Davis

And time moves forward,
And it moves back,
And slowly moves as one,
And marches fast,
The linearity,
Of time is lost,
As I lay there in,
Your arms again,
And days may be short,
But may be long,
The sun sets and rises,
And the moon goes on,
And ever come I,
To your arms again,
The moon and stars,
Of the dark night sky,
Your wandering Alice,
Down the rabbit hole,
And though I wander,
It is to you,
I always come back,
And always go,
The Hatter waiting,
For the long lost one,
My wings unfolding,
The cupboards bare,
And in your arms,
My dark night sky,
You soul my piper,
Your love my call,
To you I come back,
To you alone,
Through darkened roadways,
And paths of stone,

The Night's Sweet Embrace

Time remembered,
And time forgot,
My laughter echoes,
When I'm in your arms,
The only home,
I'll ever know,
Vagabond gypsy,
This Alice roams,
But in your arms,
I'm content and warm,
No more to wander,
Out in the storm,
Your love a beacon,
Your arms my home,
Your moon and stars,
My dark night sky.

~December 7, 2015

Bethany Davis

My Hates and My Loves

I hate to wake you, lover,
But love when you're awake,
I love to watch you sleeping,
But long for your embrace,
I love you here beside me,
Peaceful and so still,
But wait in anticipation,
Of each moment you're awake.

I hate to leave you, lover,
But love when I return,
I love our talks for hours,
But long to feel your touch,
I love each and every minute,
Each word and each long glance,
But wait in anticipation,
Of the next time we can kiss.

I hate to sit by idle,
But love to watch you cook,
I love the tastes you give me,
But can't sit still and wait,
I love to come distract you,
To hug you and to kiss,
But wait in anticipation,
For the food you make for me.

I hate the thought of leaving,
But love my soon return,
I love each time I reach you,
But hate to have to go,
I love each stolen minute,
The living and the fun,
But wait in anticipation,
Until we have to part no more.

~December 26, 2015

Bethany Davis

Blushing Girl

Bashful and shy...
　...and smiling eyes,
As I get quiet...
　...before your eyes,
Blushing girl...
　...I smile shy,
As I pull back...
　...from my desire,
As I pull back...
　...my eyes they seek,
For you to follow...
　...where I lead,
To kiss my lips...
　...and hold me tight,
Your touch my lifeline...
　...your eyes my light,
Kiss me love...
　...your bashful girl,
As I get giggly...
　...all blushing shy,
Your hands behind...
　...my leaning back,
Hold me, love...
　...and keep me close,

Bethany Davis

And with your lips...
　...on mine, delight,
You pull me back...
　...from bashful flight,
A blushing primrose...
　...so demure,
Now so delicate...
　...in this moment,
Trusting fully...
　...in my true love,
That when I pull back...
　...you'll follow me,
And this shy girl...
　...will be caught up,
In your arms...
　...that hold me close,
To kiss my lips...
　...and I open up,
The shy and bashful...
　...lost in love,
In the arms...
　...of my only love.

~January 17, 2016

How Do You Hold the Raging Wind

How do you hold the raging wind,
And calm her beating heart?
How do you make her safe, content,
Anchored to the ground?
How are you her firm firm ground,
A mountain strong and tall?
How do you hold the raging wind,
And calm her beating heart?

How do you hold the raging wind,
And calm her beating heart?
How do you bring such awesome peace,
To a raging winter storm?
How do you calm the very air,
Rushing through the trees?
How do you hold the raging wind,
And calm her beating heart?

How do you hold the raging wind,
And calm her beating heart?
How do you take that storm so wild,
And lay upon its length?
How do you hold it in your arms,
That crazy wild wind?
How do you hold the raging wind,
And calm her beating heart?

How do you hold the raging wind,
And calm her beating heart?
How do you cause her heart to yearn,
For all your tender touch?
How do you cause her pulse to start,
At every thought of you?
How do you hold the raging wind,
And calm her beating heart?

Bethany Davis

How do you hold the raging wind,
And calm her beating heart?
How is it that you speak her name,
And buds and flowers bloom?
How do you bring the calming spring,
By whispering her name?
How do you hold the raging wind,
And calm her beating heart?

How do you hold the raging wind,
And calm her beating heart?
How do you know each inner thought,
That dances through her mind?
How do you know what makes her tick,
And how to please the wind?
How do you hold the raging wind,
And calm her beating heart?

How do you hold the raging wind,
And calm her beating heart?
How do you make her smile and pine,
Each moment far from you?
How do you bring her moans and sighs,
With just your tender touch?
How do you hold the raging wind,
And calm her beating heart?

How do you hold the raging wind,
And calm her beating heart?
How do you make her safe, content,
Anchored to the ground?
How are you her firm firm ground,
A mountain strong and tall?
How do you hold the raging wind,
And calm her beating heart?

~February 20, 2016

Above All Else

There's a joy when I wake to see your face,
And to hear you before I sleep,
There is a joy when we talk while you fade,
Into that most peaceful sleep,
And little moments are all that will last,
Each one building upon the last,
And every moment I have with you,
I treasure above all else.

There's a peace when I wake wrapped in your arms,
And when I drift to sleep right there,
To hear your breathe and feel your skin,
When you're sleeping close to me,
When silence rests and we are content,
Or when we talk and laugh,
And every moment I have with you,
I treasure above all else.

There's a giggle when your eyes roam over me,
And when you say my name,
And that giggle grows from deep within,
And is my love for you,
And if I squirm and grow oh so shy,
It is your love for me,
And every moment I have with you,
I treasure above all else.

Bethany Davis

There's a tear when I leave or we are apart,
And not in your loving arms,
And the ache is like a living thing,
That can grow and make me lost,
But that tear and ache is a temporary thing,
For I always come back to you,
And every moment I have with you,
I treasure above all else.

There's a joy when I wake to see your face,
And to hear you before I sleep,
There is a joy when we talk while you fade,
Into that most peaceful sleep,
And little moments are all that will last,
Each one building upon the last,
And every moment I have with you,
I treasure above all else.

~March 28, 2016

Returning

My soul, love,
Misses,
Pines,
Longs,
Wants to return,
Seek your arms,
Your kiss,
Your touch,
Like a moth,
Flying in darkness,
Seeking,
Looking,
For just one light,
The flame,
To which it returns,
Like a creature of night,
Stuck in the light,
Sunshine and brightness,
When all it longs for is dark,
Deep,
Dark,
Night,
Starlight and moonlight,
Returning,
To the night,
The dark night,
The dark night sky,
To which it will always return,
As I will always return,
To my dark night sky.

~April 3, 2015

Bethany Davis

The Sun on Morning Dew

Through early light I journey out,
And head on down the road,
To reach my true love before sun sets,
To be in her living arms,
A journey long and hard to bear,
But worth each moment passed,
To seek my lover by the morning light,
And the sun on morning dew.

Misty morning across rivers slow,
The lazy water flows,
Open roads and field and hills,
Across all the land I go,
Tired I am each time it's done,
But glad I made the trip,
To seek my lover by the morning light,
And the sun on morning dew.

The land still sleep in the morning light,
The sun on morning dew,
Early birds that dance and sing,
The land's just waking up,
The land cries out for it feels my soul,
The longing in my heart,
To seek my lover by the morning light,
And the sun on morning dew.

Bethany Davis

Familiar roads and familiar hills,
The journey much the same,
But every time the land has changed,
As my love for her does grow,
The happy song of morning birds,
Reminds me of her laugh,
I seek my lover by the morning light,
And the sun on morning dew.

Through early light I journey out,
And head on down the road,
To reach my true love before sun sets,
To be in her living arms,
A journey long and hard to bear,
But worth each moment passed,
To seek my lover by the morning light,
And the sun on morning dew.

~August 25, 2016

On Rushing and Laziness

As I look down from high above,
And see the land below,
Lazy rivers meandering,
In their journey across the plains,
A sleepy land in morning sun,
A land that knows no rush,
And think about my rushing on,
As I go to seek my love.

The journey's filled with many things,
With both rushing and worrying,
Like this plane soars like a hurried thing,
So high above the plains,
But when I'm there and in her arms,
And all is right again,
No rushing comes as we live and breathe,
Me and my loving love.

We each must act to then relax,
And relax before we act,
And the rush must come, like a hawk in hunt,
Before we lay as one,
Even on the plains, the sleepy plains,
The hawk and prey must rush,
But when it's done peace must return,
Like me in my lover's arms.

And lazy rivers and lazy hills,
Are not always what they seem,
And rush must come, and rush must go,
For lazy times to come,
And the morning dew is a land alive,
As the birds flit around for food,
And I rush along in my journey long,
As I go to seek my love.

~August 25, 2016

Bethany Davis

The Twilit Lands

Through the fields,
  of green grass and flowers,
    in the twilit lands I roam,
Lost in shadows,
  and cracks of light,
    meandering in my mind,
Eternal night,
  so close and far,
    and stars that ever shine,
Forever wandering,
  your Alice roams,
    in wonderlands and mist.

In wonderlands,
  your Alice roams,
    in twilit lands afar,
And in shadowed lands,
  that are only lit,
    by elusive cracks of light,
But your love,
  and your voice,
    forever leads me home,
A lantern shining,
  in the darkest night,
    the Night that is my love.

Bethany Davis

The Night you are,
  where my stars and moon,
    shine in twilit lands,
Your whispered voice,
  it calls me home,
    through elusive cracks of light,
The cupboard doors,
  now open wide,
    and me now finally home,
For in your arms,
  my dark night sky,
    I'm safe and found, secure.

~September 26, 2016

By Dawn's Golden Light

My flight takes off,
  by the light of dawn,
    as the sun just now appears,
There's solace found,
  in the new day's light,
    in the healing wind of Dawn,
Her light shines on,
  with a golden glow,
    like the silver of the moon,
And reminds that,
  I'll come again,
    to my baby's loving arms.

The golden light,
  brings a different view,
    than the night scape when I did land,
The night before,
  when I was so worn,
    from the journey and the pain,
My missingness,
  seems slightly less,
    in the golden cracks of Dawn,
But the ache remains,
  that I felt at night,
    first night not in my baby's arms.

Bethany Davis

The missing is,
  a living thing,
    that changes as it grows,
Sometime the pain,
  is oh so great,
    others it seems to ebb,
But the tempering,
  of Dawn's new light,
    is really just to hide,
The pain that aches,
  deep in my soul,
    Away from my baby's arms.

~October 10, 2016

Your Embrace

I miss you so,
With every breath,
And long for your embrace,
You are my heart,
You are my soul,
You are my everything.

And as I age,
I want to be,
With you for every day,
If I turn grey,
If my body hurts,
No difference it will make.

With all my days,
And all my years,
I will always be at your side,
Hold me love,
In night and day,
I long for your embrace.

~October 16, 2016

Bethany Davis

In From the Cold

To be in that bed tonight,
And be there in your loving arms,
It seems so long til morning comes,
And I can seek your warmth,
The nights are cold and long,
When I work while you do sleep,
I long to come in from the cold,
And curl up with you.

To be in that bed tonight,
And be there in your loving arms,
The nights stretch on like ages past,
In the wasteland far from you,
Each hour passes with you so near,
And still so out of reach,
I long to come in from the cold,
And curl up with you.

To be in that bed tonight,
And be there in your loving arms,
The house it feels to different now,
When I return to find you there,
My baby's arms they hold me tight,
Like the sky hold the moon and stars,
I long to come in from the cold,
And curl up with you.

Bethany Davis

To be in that bed tonight,
And be there in your loving arms,
My baby dreams when I'm here at work,
But holds me when I'm not,
The nights are long with you so near,
But the coming home is bliss,
I long to come in from the cold,
And curl up with you.

To be in that bed tonight,
And be there in your loving arms,
Oh how I wish I could leave right now,
And come home to amazing you,
But hours it is until I can,
And days or months or more,
I long to come in from the cold,
And curl up with you.

To be in that bed tonight,
And be there in your loving arms,
It seems so long til morning comes,
And I can seek your warmth,
The nights are cold and long,
When I work while you do sleep,
I long to come in from the cold,
And curl up with you.

~December 26, 2016

In the Morning Light

As shadows spread across the hills,
And the sun so slowly disappears,
The mountain shadows spread across,
As Night spreads her feathered wings,
I know my lover's here at home,
Not a thousand klicks away,
And in the morning light.

Night's shadows form and keep me safe,
And wrap around my soul,
When darkness dances all around,
And fills the great wide sky,
The dark night sky that spreads her arms,
To hold the moon and stars,
Both in the darkness of the night,
And in the morning light.

The stillness of the winter night,
The way the air hangs still,
Or moves with rushing mighty wind,
That could push a person down,
In stillness or in raging wind,
The night watches and it waits,
As I wait to come home to her,
Soon in the morning light.

~December 27, 2016

Bethany Davis

Memories Stolen From Time

I miss you, love.
Memories are only so much,
  even amazing ones.
I miss your touch,
  your arms,
    your voice,
      your gentleness.
I miss each little movement,
  each little look,
    each little inside joke,
      each little moment,
        stolen from time,
          ours forever,
            a memory but much more,
            infinite,
              ours.

~January 1, 2017

Bethany Davis

That Book That Has Never Been Written

That book you mention,
That book,
That's never been written,
That book,
Traced across your heart,
Across my heart,
Across our hearts,
Our love,
The passion and fury,
The tears and giggles,
All the depths of it,
All the muchness,
Your muchness,
My muchness,
Our muchness,
So amazing,
So full of laughter,
So full of pain,
So full of wonder,
So full of muchness,
Muchness,
Always,
Like the moon and stars,
Alone with the dark night sky,
Nothing else,
Eternal,
Forever,
Like the endless breadth of the Abyss,
The Outer Dark,
But so much more,

Bethany Davis

Sunlight through cracks of light,
Reflected off shards of tea cups,
The colour of darkness,
Stretching forever,
Onward,
Upward,
Outward,
Inward,
Into our deepest depths,
Where dreams and nightmares dance hand in hand,
In the shadowy halflight,
Twilight,
Shadowed,
Unknowing,
Yet known too well,
Too deeply,
The muchness,
Rich and strong,
Overwhelming yet intoxicating,
You say the moon cries sometimes,
The tears lost in the wind and streams,
Streaming down,
Like rain from a raging storm,
Or like the gentle rain of a spring shower,
Now a raging torrent,
Swirling darkness,
Swirling emotion,
Out of control,
Endless,
But now,
A gentle shower,
Spring beauty,
Rebirth,
Life returning,
Cracks of sunlight,
Dappled light,
Smiles and giggles,
All pretense,
All worry,
All pain,
Forgotten in the moment,

The Night's Sweet Embrace

Lost in laughter,
The tears,
Like dew,
A gentle muchness,
And all this,
Wrapped up in our love,
Like the stars,
The stars you say are so, so bright,
The stars you just want to gather,
Gather into your arms,
And hold oh so tight,
Your moon and stars,
Lost in your muchness,
Your arms,
Wrapped around me,
Holding me,
Holding all my muchness,
The muchness of the moon and stars,
Lost in the muchness of the dark night sky,
Your Alice,
Lost in your wonderland,
The wonderland that is you,
Your muchness,
That book,
Traced across both our hearts,
That book,
Which has never been written.

~January 29, 2017

Bethany Davis

A Ring Around the Moon, My Love

A ring around the moon, my love,
Is like your arms around your girl,
You hold me close and keep me safe,
And I shine because you do,
I feel so safe in your loving arms,
When you hold me oh so tight,
For a ring around the moon, my love,
Is like your arms around your girl.

A ring around the moon, my love,
Is like your love around my heart,
You love me so and keep me safe,
And I'll always love you, too,
I feel your love with all my heart,
And my heart cries out to yours,
For a ring around the moon, my love,
Is like your love around my heart.

A ring around the moon, my love,
Is like the look there in your eyes,
I see your love, sometimes your lust,
All the time you look at me,
I giggle, love, under your gaze,
And squirm but I delight,
For a ring around the moon, my love,
Is like the look there in your eyes.

~February 5, 2017

Bethany Davis

Simple Words

When my last words before you sleep,
And your last words back to me,
Are those simple words that mean so much,
From my lips or from your own,
As you fade into restful sleep,
And I go back to work,
Those simple words, I love you,
Leave me smiling in the night.

When my last words before we sleep,
And your last words back to me,
Are those simple words that mean so much,
And our lips seal them with a kiss,
As we both fade into restful sleep,
To dream in loving arms,
Those simple words, I love you,
Leave me smiling while I sleep.

When my last words before I sleep,
And your last words back to me,
Are those simple words that mean so much,
As I send you off with a kiss,
As I fade back into restful sleep,
And you head off to work,
Those simple words, I love you,
Leave me smiling while I sleep.

~February 8, 2017

Bethany Davis

By the Gate

I wait by the gate,
  to fly once more,
Toward your waiting arms.

I wait because,
  it is a must,
To kiss your lips once more.

Each delay,
  is a heavy thing,
For I long so much for you.

But all the time,
  and all delays,
Are worth it to be held by you.

The airport chairs,
  have seen a thousand waits,
Not just my waiting now.

The hopes and dreams.
  of each waiting one,
They are heavy yet floaty things.

And like your love,
  each waiting one,
Finally flew on out.

And I will fly,
  when the time is full,
Toward your waiting arms.

~February 8, 2017

Bethany Davis

Doubting Planes

There is that point it seems to hesitate,
Each time a plane takes off,
It seems there are doubts that remain,
Though the plane's flight has just begun,
Just like the plane when it hesitates,
I do when I spread my wings,
When I fly upon their strength,
I'm never quite sure I can.

You tell me love that I have wings,
And I know that is the truth,
You tell me that I can surely fly,
And you're right, I surely can,
But my doubts my love I hesitate,
Just as the plane also seems to do,
But I know I can and know I do,
Why then do I doubt it, love?

But your faith it speaks to me,
Your faith my wings will hold,
I know not why you care so much,
To lend me your faith in me,
I am strong I know my love,
Though I seldom do believe,
But my strength it is lifted up,
When you tell me what you think.

You see me love more clear that I,
Will ever see or know myself,
You know my strength and you know my wings,
And when you say it I can surely fly,
Above the clouds just like that plane,
Which pushes through its doubts,
And brings me love to your waiting arms,
You help me find my wings.

~February 8, 2017

Bethany Davis

The Moment of Waking

The moment of waking,
  So sweet,
    So peaceful,
      Like a fire on a winter day,
        Like a cool breeze in summer,
Slowly coming forth,
  Returning,
    Leaving dream,
      Awareness returning in the shadows,
        Understanding,
          Where I am,
I awake and nestle close,
  Safe and secure,
    Held,
      Oh so tight,
        Like a thing treasured,
          Something you don't want to let go,
            Someone you don't want to let go,

Me,
 There in your arms,
  The awareness of half waking,
   The sweetness of embrace,
    Me,
     Held in your arms,
      Held to your breast,
       You hold me so close,
Your hand,
 Gentle clutching my breast,
  Legs entwined,
   Your breath on my neck,
    In the shadowy light of night,
     The shadowy light of early morning,
      Like moonlight through clouds,
       Starlight not quite seen,
Waking,
 Your moon and stars,
  Held firmly,
   Gently,
    Lovingly,
     In the loving arms,
      The gentle arms,
       The safe and secure arms,
        Of my dark night sky.

~February 10, 2017

It's Worth It

It's worth it, love,
  All of this,
    Each time I come to you,
All the crowds,
  All the mess,
    And all the fucking flux,
It's hard sometimes,
  The mess gets bad,
    And your baby gets so grumbly,
But all the crowds,
  All the mess,
    And all the fucking flux,
It's worth it, love,
  To come to you,
    To feel your kiss and touch,
All the flux,
  All the mess,
    All the fucking crowds,
I'll walk through them,
  I'll go the miles,
    If they lead me to your door,
It's worth it, love,
  Worth it all,
    Worth the pain and flux,
Just to be,
  There in your arms,
    For each moment that I can,
It's worth it love,
  It's so worth it,
    It's so fucking worth it all.

~February 18, 2017

Bethany Davis

The Moon on My Right

Finally flying, but away from you,
The moon always on my right,
Through the sky faster than any horse,
Eastward I'm finally bound,
Oh for return to your sweet embrace,
Instead of far away,
But movement is a better thing,
That the static waiting flux.

The time we spent, I treasure, love,
Each moment and every kiss,
The hours and days we spent this time,
And each visit before this one,
The longer trips, the partings, love,
Are harder than the shorter ones,
And though I'm glad to be on my way,
Staying would be better still.

The flux is hard when I cannot move,
When all is struggling plight,
In the air or driving, love,
Is much easier to bare,
And though the moon is on my right,
And the east Sun at my fore,
I'm glad I'm moved on the journey home,
Instead of stuck is Saskatoon.

Bethany Davis

But better still, my heart, my soul,
If I was returning now to you,
Your loving arms, your yearning fire,
The love we each do share,
I miss my heart, my soul, my song,
When I'm flying away from Saskatchewan,
Oh for the hour when we stand,
And the partings are then no more.

Finally flying, but away from you,
The moon always on my right,
Through the sky faster than any horse,
Eastward I'm finally bound,
Oh for return to your sweet embrace,
Instead of far away,
But movement is a better thing,
That the static waiting flux.

~February 18, 2017

Dancing Through Thoughts and Memories

Dancing thoughts and memories,
Go round and round my head,
Thoughts of you my lover dark,
And memories of your touch,
I long for you on winter nights,
And in the summer heat,
I long for just one fleeting kiss,
And your breath there on my neck.

Each night is long when we're apart,
And hours stretch out like days,
My thoughts they wander ever on,
Through memories and dreams,
Thoughts of you like fleeting birds,
Or like deer in a thicket stand,
I feel so lost like a ship at sea,
In an endless torrent storm.

I long my love for that fine day,
When I'm always by your side,
And tender words and gentle touch,
Fill the darkness of every night,
I sigh so loud as I think and dream,
Of that day I know will come,
When we kiss good night, but not good bye,
And lay in each other's arms.

~February 27, 2017

Bethany Davis

My Lover Sleeps

My lover sleeps so far away,
In the bed we often share,
I dream of her while I'm awake,
With my eyes still open wide,
I long to be there by her side,
And to cuddle in her arms,
The moon and stars so closely held,
By the loving dark night sky.

My lover sleeps so far away,
While I am up and about,
I long for her in the deep of night,
Long for her sweet embrace,
I hope and pray she's sleeping sound,
In peace and restful dreams,
Of the moon and stars closely held,
By the loving dark night sky.

My lover sleeps so far away,
Where I so want to be,
Her arms I crave and her touch,
Her kiss and her sweet caress,
Memories and thoughts at night,
The longing for my butch,
For the moon and stars to be closely held,
By the loving dark night sky.

~March 5, 2017

Bethany Davis

Bitter Water

Sometimes the loneliness rises up,
Like a foundation from deep within,
Bitter water that is hard to drink,
But the only thing there is,
It's not a loneliness of all alone,
It's a very different thing,
It's the loneliness that can only come,
From missing the one I love.

The missing wells up both now and then,
Though I try to hold it down,
To keep the fountain from rising up,
To keep the flood doors closed,
The pressure builds deep in my soul,
It builds and builds and builds,
Until it ruptures through the walls,
And brings forth torrential rains.

Those rains that fall from both my eyes,
Those rains I've come to know,
That flow forth from that missingness,
Of not being there in your arms,
The rain, my love, that flows from me,
That falls with every single tear,
Are just the tip of the water there,
The loneliness my soul knows well.

~May 23, 2017

Bethany Davis

A World Apart

Your arms around me from behind,
As you hold me to your breasts,
The smile that forms as we stand that way,
And my joyful and contented sigh,
It's peace, my love, within your arms,
Whether standing or bare in bed,
A world apart that's just us two,
When I'm in your loving arms.

You kiss my neck or whisper, love,
Right there in my waiting ear,
Your voice that is a song to me,
That sets my heart ablaze,
You kiss is fierce and full of love,
Lightning shooting through my soul,
A world apart that's just us two,
When I'm in your loving arms.

Your hands move up across my breasts,
And they linger for just a bit,
Hands so deft that know my curves,
Know just how to move and touch,
The tenderness but firm and strong,
Making my hips move against you, love,
A world apart that's just us two,
When I'm in your loving arms.

Higher still your hands do move,
My shoulders are now in reach,
And slide my dress right off my arms,
To fall in a puddle at our feet,
Your breasts, my love, against my back,
Me wishing they were bare,
A world apart that's just us two,
When I'm in your loving arms.

Bethany Davis

Slowly, love, I turn around,
Still in your loving arms,
A kiss we share so full of lust,
Yet so full of tender love,
My arms around my lover dark,
Her arms still holding me,
A world apart that's just us two,
When I'm in your loving arms.

My hands go down to raise your shirt,
And toss it to the side,
Your breasts are bare against my chest,
Mine bare against your own,
Your pants they fall, I take your hand,
And lead you to the bed,
A world apart that's just us two,
When I'm in your loving arms.

Your arms around me in our bed,
As you hold me to your breasts,
The kiss we share of passioned lust,
Of a love beyond all else,
Enjoy, my love, my body fair,
And I'll enjoy yours above all else,
A world apart that's just us two,
When I'm in your loving arms.

~May 23, 2017

Eternal Love

Eternal love,
My lover dark,
Down endless halls of time,
The dance we share,
Beyond the veil,
The weave and warp and weft,
My soul cries out,
And always seeks,
Your own my lover dark,
And all my days,
I long for you,
And seek you in the night.

The pain my love,
Each time we part,
Is worth the joy we find,
Each time I come,
To your warm arms,
And lay down at your side,
Each time I go,
I always return,
For I crave you lover dark,
Your arms are where,
I'm meant to be,
In the darkness of the night.

Bethany Davis

Feel my soul,
And feel my heart,
How they long for only you,
Know my love,
And know my joy,
And know how I miss you so,
The eternal halls,
We have always walked,
Always lead back to us,
I love you love,
Both night and day,
I love my dark night sky.

~June 24, 2017

Travel Worn

Tired now,
Of travel wear,
As I travel home,
Longing now,
For my love,
As I fly the other way,
Want of home,
With you or not,
But with you would be such bliss,
Tired now,
Of travel wear,
As I travel home.

Weary now,
From all before,
From flying here and there,
Wayworn soul,
And weathered mind,
Longing for your arms,
To a bed,
To mine or yours,
But yours would be such bliss,
Weary now,
From all before,
From flying here and there.

Bethany Davis

All the time,
This time with you,
More of late than before,
Spoiled me,
For want of you,
I wish time had no end,
To home I go,
To mine not yours,
Oh for you to come with me,
All the time,
This time with you,
More of late than before.

Oh my love,
My only one,
The one for which I pine,
My weary soul,
My wayworn heart,
Longs for your loving arms,
Want of home,
That is your arms,
The place that is such bliss,
Oh my love,
My only one,
The one for which I pine.

~August 4, 2017

Rising in the Eerie Sky

The moon,
So close to full,
Rising in an eerie sky,
A misty sky,
A sky that glows with the lights of town,
Like the fire glow,
Of a welcoming campfire,
Welcoming,
Like your arms,
Holding me tight,
Where I belong,
But like the moon,
Like the glowing sky,
Like the few stars that dare to pierce the mist,
Like the campfire,
Glowing through the trees,
Your waiting arms,
Far away,
But close in memory,
As close as your voice,
Your words,
In my ears,
Bringing comfort,
Longing for touch,
Happy for speech,

Bethany Davis

Your love,
Through your words,
Through your soul,
Through our entwined spirts,
Your love,
Holding me close,
Safe,
Even when arms are far away,
Like the white moon,
In the glowing sky,
But I can touch the moon,
I am your moon,
And even far away,
I can feel you,
My dark night sky,
Holding your moon and stars,
Like that dark night sky,
Beyond the mist,
That sky that holds those stars,
Bravely peeking through,
That sky that holds that moon,
So close to full,
Rising in the eerie sky.

~September 2, 2017

A Sliver Moon

A sliver moon in dark blue sky,
  Just before the coming dawn,
    Just before the coming end,
      Of one more lunar month,
        A white shining parenthesis,
      In a slowly waxing sky,
  Alone with just the morning star,
The bringer of the dawn.

The arc and point in dark blue sky,
  So beautiful to behold,
    The moon and star held there still,
      By the eternal dark night sky,
        As the growing dawn hides the night,
      And the earth-shade hides the moon,
  Alone with just the morning star,
The bringer of the dawn.

As night sky fades into growing dawn,
  The moon and morning star do too,
    Just like I fade into your arms,
      When we both head to sleep,
        And wakefulness fades in joyful sleep,
      And your arms they hold me close,
  Alone with just my lover true,
At night or in the dawn.

~September 17, 2017

Bethany Davis

What Are the Stars?

What are the stars,
  my love, my heart,
Without the dark night sky?
The stars they fade,
  when comes the dawn,
Just as the night sky does,
And as they fade,
  they do not shine,
As if they cease to be,
Like I would fade,
  my love, my heart,
Without your loving arms.

Your loving arms,
  my love, my heart,
They hold my heart and soul,
Like the shining stars,
  that are so held,
By that endless dark night sky,
Your love my love,
  it calls my soul,
Like the starry sky above,
Please hold me close,
  my love, my heart,
Within your loving arms.

Bethany Davis

It is your love,
  my love, my heart,
What makes me shine so bright,
Just like the night,
  the dark night sky,
Brings forth the shining stars,
When we're apart,
  I fade away,
Like the stars do in the dawn,
It's only you,
  my love, my heart,
It is your loving arms.

What are the stars,
  my love, my heart,
Without the dark night sky?
The stars they fade,
  when comes the dawn,
Just as the night sky does,
And as they fade,
  they do not shine,
As if they cease to be,
Like I would fade,
  my love, my heart,
Without your loving arms.

~September 24, 2017

The Miles Speed By

The miles speed by,
Like the minutes do,
Adding ever upward,
The steady beat,
Like your heart pulse,
Of time and space apart,
By car and plane,
But the wrong way,
Away from your loving arms,
I crave you love,
More than all else,
To be back there again.

Distance passes,
And time goes by,
But my love ever strong,
My longing grows,
For your soft touch,
I know the distance hurts,
Please dream of me,
And for the day,
When the parting will end,
I crave you love,
More than all else,
To be back there again.

~October 13, 2017

Bethany Davis

Southward Bound

Across the prairies rolling by,
In late summer or in the fall,
Flaming colours of changing leaves,
Against golden grains below,
The sky so blue it seems surreal,
The expanse that spreads across,
Southward bound to your arms,
My love, my only one.

The anxious birds that look around,
They feel the time draws near,
And gather close to other birds,
Other anxious flocking ones,
Not quite time for them to go,
But they feel it in the winds,
But I'm southward bound to your arms,
My love, my only one.

Fields now dry as harvest rolls,
And the geese that gather there,
And in the lakes and sloughs abound,
Coming down from further north,
They have not passed on by us here,
But they've started the journey south,
Like I'm southward bound to your arms,
My love, my only one.

Each time we part is very hard,
But each time I come to you,
It's worth the time and journeying,
It's worth any price I could pay,
To come to you like ribboned geese,
Across the prairies rolling by,
Southward bound to your arms,
My love, my only one.

~October 17, 2017

Bethany Davis

The Myriad Missing Mist

I drift upon a sea of mist,
In the shadowed time of night,
Awake and drifting as at sea,
While you are at home asleep,
The misty sea we know quite well,
That we cross and cross again,
The myriad missing that is the mist,
And I'm missing you once again.

The sea is dark, my love, my soul,
Into the depths I cannot see,
What creatures lurk below my sight,
The fears and the hopes and dreams,
Lost at sea like a wayward ship,
Your arms are the port I crave,
The myriad missing that is the mist,
And I'm missing you once again.

The sea of time where we've travelled far,
On which we part and we then return,
The ages pass and minutes more,
Each day seems like all eternity,
The longing's strong and makes me pine,
For just one so simple touch,
The myriad missing that is the mist,
And I'm missing you once again.

Bethany Davis

And in the shadows of the night,
When most everyone does dream,
Like dreaming mist my memories,
Do sing of your arms my love,
The shadows dance just like my soul,
For the memories of your touch,
The myriad missing that is the mist,
And I'm missing you once again.

Alone I sail as I pine for you,
The sea of mist stretches wide,
To find the shores that are your arms,
Where I lay in sweetest peace,
Soon, my love, and the wait will fade,
And the parting and returning cease,
The mist long gone but as for now,
Yes I'm missing you once again.

~October 23, 2017

Neon Code

Neon text,
Code,
Forming,
Reworking,
A field of black,
Black box,
Code,
In neon colours,
In a black window,
A laptop,
So small,
Paper thin,
Almost,
She types away,
Lost in code,
Beside cables,
Devices charging,
Across the way,
Pictures dance,
Video,
Streaming,
Dancing,
A movie theatre,
All wrapped up,
Wrapped in a laptop,
The man gazing,
Intent,
Lost in images,
On a carpeted floor,

Bethany Davis

Beside,
Above,
The chair beside him,
A phone,
So small,
Like something from a movie,
But now common place,
Social media,
Friends,
Acquaintances,
Strangers,
Across the world,
In the palm of her hand,
Lost in words,
On an airport chair,
Tablets,
Laptops,
Phones,
Devices,
A thousand devices,
Each more powerful,
Than computers that used to fill rooms,
Bits streaming,
Flowing,
Through the air,
Wireless,
Connecting,
To an invisible world,
Stretching,

The Night's Sweet Embrace

Around the world,
Like airplanes,
Connecting distant shores,
The airport a laptop,
A phone,
A tablet,
Each airport a device,
Connected by plane flight,
Through the air,
Wireless,
Each person,
Flowing,
Moving,
Connecting,
A thousand people,
A thousand bits,
Kilobits,
People,
Each moving to their destination,
Data flowing,
Carrying information,
Memories,
Each person,
With their own memories,
Own knowledge,
Own purpose,
Flowing,
Connecting,

Bethany Davis

Like messages in social media,
Like a movie streamed,
Like code written and sent,
Synced,
A never ending flow,
The data slows,
The data ebbs,
The data wanes,
But,
It waxes,
It flows,
It hastens,
Just like the people,
Sometimes few,
Sometimes slow moving,
Sometimes fast moving,
Sometimes huge crowds,
Ever coming,
Ever going,
And here I sit,
Amongst data and people,
Devices and memories,
Chairs and planes,
As I wait to fly once more,
On more bit,
Like so many others,
But no others,
None of this sea of bits and people,
No one else,
Knows your loving arms.

~October 23, 2017

Like Falling Leaves

Inspired by the words of my Sophia.

Each moment,
 Changing,
  The flux moves,
   Twists,
   Dances,
  Time's dance,
 With twinning motion,
  Round and round,
 Like falling leaves.

Leaves we are,
 Falling downward,
  Falling ever slowly,
Floating downward,
 Lucky we are,
  Like falling leaves.

Each moment,
 Suspended,
   The flux spins,
    Turns,
    Weaves,
   Time's tapestry,
  The warp and weft,
   Over and over,
  Like falling leaves.

Bethany Davis

Leaves we are,
 Falling downward,
  Falling ever slowly,
Floating downward,
 Lucky we are,
  Like falling leaves.

Each moment,
 Remembered,
  The flux recalls,
   Echoes,
   Resounds,
  Time's hall,
 Vibrating silence,
  Over and over,
Like falling leaves.

Leaves we are,
 Falling downward,
  Falling ever slowly,
Floating downward,
 Lucky we are,
  Like falling leaves.

The Night's Sweet Embrace

Each moment,
　Consuming,
　　The flux within,
　　　Embrace,
　　　Touching,
　　Time's promise,
　You and me,
　　Over and over,
Like falling leaves.

Leaves we are,
　Falling downward,
　　Falling ever slowly,
Floating downward,
　Lucky we are,
　　Like falling leaves.

Each moment,
　Our loving,
　　The flux and peace,
　　　Your skin,
　　　My skin,
　　Time's dance,
　　Over and over,
Like falling leaves.

~November 6, 2017

Bethany Davis

Soon

Soon my love I can hold you close,
And kiss you in the dark,
Feel your touch and feel your skin,
There in your loving arms,
The craving grows as each night is past,
And with the dusk of each new day,
My dark night sky I love you so,
And the love inside me grows.

Your kiss my love is like a dream,
The memory hanging on,
That you try so hard to grasp ahold,
As your sleep does fade away,
Each kiss you give upon my lips,
Or on my naked skin,
I store away in sweet memory's hold,
And the love inside me grows.

Your touch my love is a thing of awe,
That delights me in the night,
Under the sun or under the stars,
In day as well as night,
A sweet caress with just a touch,
Butterflies flutter deep within,
Your touch is such a treasured thing,
And the love inside me grows.

Bethany Davis

Your arms my love when they hold me close,
So safe at home secure,
A thousand words in a thousand verses,
Not even a poem is quite enough,
The loving arms of the dark night sky,
She holds the moon and stars,
A thing that's so very beyond all words,
And the love inside me grows.

Soon my love I can hold you close,
And kiss you in the dark,
Feel your touch and feel your skin,
There in your loving arms,
The craving grows as each night is past,
And with the dusk of each new day,
My dark night sky I love you so,
And the love inside me grows.

~February 4, 2018

Each Day

Each day that passes when we're apart,
Is harder than the day before,
Longing and missing are living things,
That keep growing as time goes by,
Your loving arms that hold me so tight,
I long for them through each new day,
To have known your touch but be so far,
Makes me pine for you even more.

The fears and worries like persistent birds,
Such clamour in my thoughts and mind,
I lock them away safe and so secure,
In cages so they'll give me peace,
Still emotions flow like a torrent strong,
And bring about a storm of tears,
To have known your touch but be so far,
Makes me pine for you even more.

It's easier love to hold onto hope,
Than to face the fears and tears,
None as great as the fear of losing you,
O my heart and my soul and song,
For I want our time and I want our life,
To wake each morning in your arms,
To have known your touch but be so far,
Makes me pine for you even more.

Bethany Davis

There's an ache in my heart each time we part,
And a flutter each time we talk,
And I long for you as the days go by,
Longing rises from deep within,
It's so hard to wait both for you and me,
And to trust in others' say,
To have known your touch but be so far,
Makes me pine for you even more.

Each day that passes when we're apart,
Is harder than the day before,
Longing and missing are living things,
That keep growing as time goes by,
Your loving arms that hold me so tight,
I long for them through each new day,
To have known your touch but be so far,
Makes me pine for you even more.

~March 30, 2018

Passing Time

Passing time as days go by,
And I miss you oh so much,
Longing grows each new day,
As the time at last grows short,
I pine and yearn for that place,
Soon I will be there my love,
In the only place that I feel safe,
In my only home, your arms.

Months have passed, my only love
And each one has been so hard,
The missing grew and pining too,
With us so very far apart,
But I come to you so very soon,
In days not weeks or months,
To spend the time up at our lake,
And my only home, your arms.

The summer heat that is so hard,
Is nothing compared to this,
The passing time since last we kissed,
The weeks and months that passed,
Your kiss my love that makes me weak,
I long for your lips and tongue,
And for that place I long to be,
In my only home, your arms.

Bethany Davis

Soon I fly through soaring skies,
Soon I make my way to you,
The journey that I know so well,
That's always worth the time,
The journey that calls me to you,
In body as well as heart,
Takes me to the place I love,
To my only home, your arms.

Passing time as days go by,
And I miss you oh so much,
Longing grows each new day,
As the time at last grows short,
I pine and yearn for that place,
Soon I will be there my love,
In the only place that I feel safe,
In my only home, your arms.

~June 14, 2018

So How Long Can?

So how long can,
The moon and stars,
Be without the dark night sky,
And wander on,
Lost and alone,
In the grey forgotten mist?
Wrong it is,
To wander so,
Without that endlessness,
The dark night sky,
That spreads beyond,
Where the moon and stars belong.

So how long can,
The emptiness,
That echoes in my soul,
Be never full,
When we're apart,
When I long for you so much?
Each lonely night,
Is oh so hard,
In the pining hours long,
Hours that should,
Be in your arms,
Where my lonely soul belongs.

Bethany Davis

So how long can,
The dark night sky,
Be empty of moon and stars,
With arms that should,
Hold them so tight,
Instead of longing to have them there?
The misty nights,
Like the chasm deep,
The time and distance long,
Before I come,
To your warm arms,
The moon and stars of the dark night sky.

So how long can,
The greyness last,
In the swirling mists of time,
Before I come,
Now very close,
But when it's been so very very long?
But now I come,
The time has come,
For my sojourn away to end,
The parting mists,
The greyness ends,
Now is how long it can.

~June 14, 2018

Liquid Gold

Liquid gold across snow-strewn hills,
At ten thousand feet above,
Poured forth like fire on perfect white,
Molten lava of living gold,
The white white hills so golden lit,
Whipped up by stirring wind,
A landscape spread so high above,
All the many worlds below.

The gold it flares like burning fire,
And then it fades to blue,
That twilight blue like shadowed snow,
A blue that knows no peer,
In blue-grey shadows under pale blue sky,
Sky variegated and rainbow hewed,
A landscape spread so high above,
All the many worlds below.

Rising mists as we descend,
Into those snow-strewn hills,
Cutting through like a shaking knife,
As the hills they take us in,
Like hollow hills beneath rolling snow,
As we slowly pass on down,
Through a landscape spread so high above,
All the many worlds below.

To you my love I slowly come down,
Back to the ground below,
To travel south but a little more,
To find your waiting arms,
The home I know so safe secure,
A delight beyond all words,
More than landscapes spread so high above,
All the many worlds below.

~June 17, 2018

Bethany Davis

Those Depths That Rise So High

Your love, my love, I feel so strong,
  like a wave inside my soul,
That rises up like a roaring tide,
  and moves all there is of me,
I feel so strong your every breath,
  and each word you ever say,
Like the moon that pulls upon the tide,
  your love pulls upon my soul.

A thousand stars with the moon before,
  might be my raging tide,
But the dark night sky is vaster still,
  those depths that rise so high,
Each star that's me and each pale moon beam,
  is held there within your soul,
And all the lights in the dark night sky,
  are but a candle in the night.

The Night's Sweet Embrace

Your depths, my love, they call to me,
  and pull me ever on,
Toward your love, your heart, your soul,
  toward all that is my love,
That I would know your love, my love,
  and be held by the dark night sky,
Is greater than all that ever was,
  and all that will ever be.

I long that I would know all your depths,
  know more with each passing day,
As we learn each other from the outside in,
  each day and month and year,
The journey, love, like the roaming wind,
  will never find an end,
And onward in and to the depths,
  each day, each month, each year.

~September 14, 2018

Bethany Davis

This Journey to the North

To have you, love, here by my side,
On this journey to the North,
To have you close in this empty seat,
Left open for you alone,
To hold your hand or touch you knee,
To see you smiling there,
Oh I long to have you by my side,
On this journey to the North.

Each moment, love, apart from you,
Is like the restless empty sea,
The surface waves hide so much,
That waits below the pale,
I try so hard to stay so calm,
And not let the longing grow,
But I long to have you by my side,
On this journey to the North.

Your depths, my love, are like the sea,
Unknowable but by me,
I dive so deep I want for air,
It's worth all I have to give,
Each moment, love, like each wave,
Is a treasure to my heart,
Oh I long to have you by my side,
On this journey to the North.

The Night's Sweet Embrace

Please know, my love, and please believe,
How much I love you so,
The way my heart and soul cry out,
And long for all of you,
You'll never know how much you mean,
And how strong my love for you,
Oh I long to have you by my side,
On this journey to the North.

I'm northward bound, my love, my soul,
And wish it was to you,
I'm glad to go and journey forth,
To see my family there,
But my soul does long the further on,
For you and only you,
Oh I long to have you by my side,
On this journey to the North.

To have you, love, here by my side,
On this journey to the North,
To have you close in this empty seat,
Left open for you alone,
To hold your hand or touch you knee,
To see you smiling there,
Oh I long to have you by my side,
On this journey to the North.

~September 1, 2018

Bethany Davis

I Missed You So

I've missed you so up in the north,
For we had so little time,
I haven't seen the face I love,
In far too many days,
I'm glad we had the time to call,
And glad I made this trip,
But I miss you so, my heart, my soul,
I miss you with all my soul.

I'm sorry I made the trip alone,
I wish you'd been with me,
To share the wonders of the north,
In more than photography,
To hold your hands and kiss your lips,
To sleep in your loving arms,
I miss you so, my heart, my soul,
The missing a dreadful ache.

My thoughts are always on my love,
And missing you is strong,
As I wish you could see all the sites,
And experience all with me,
And watch me play or join with us,
With the kids whom brought me joy,
I share what I can but wish for more,
Wish for your loving touch.

To lay, my love, in your loving arms,
Whether in tropics or arctic cold,
To share each moment by your side,
I long for you so strong,
It's hard, my love, to keep unlost,
When I long for you so much,
And hard to write through longing tears,
A poem for my love and life.

Bethany Davis

I love you so, I want you to know,
I miss you every single day,
You are so far and I try to hide,
To pretend it's all okay,
But no my love it's really not,
I miss you oh so much,
And there's only so long,
I can keep it caged,
And not speak or write the words.

In poems, love, I get so lost,
When the longing is so strong,
And I crave you more than anything,
And want so to lay in your loving arms,
For you to hold me is the bliss I crave,
More than any other thing,
And it is hard, so very hard,
Even my poetry can't say.

I have no words that really say,
In verse, poetry, or prose,
What you mean to me, my love,
I get lost trying to form the words,
And all the words, like all the years,
Pile up and seem long but short,
And make not a lick of any sense,
Except inside my raging thoughts.

And I ramble on in poetry,
And know not what I say,
Through longing tears,
And longing strong,
And craving for your arms.

And form it breaks and words do too,
As the plane descends to home,
A home that isn't where you are,
So a home that is incomplete.

The Night's Sweet Embrace

Forgive me, love, for breaking down,
For my missing overwhelmed,
I know not if my poetry,
Is in English or Bethanese.

I hope, my love, you'll understand,
And know my heart and soul,
Know what I mean and know my heart,
that misses you so much,
And I ramble on and do not know,
If my poem shows my heart,
But I long for you,
I long so hard,
For your soul,
Your touch,
Your smile.

It's hard my love as I descend,
Back to Colorado's land,
To know I will still be apart,
From your arms and lips and hands,
I hope you know the power you have,
With just a little touch,
A brush of loving fingertips,
Like a kiss upon my skin.

And know my love you are my life,
I'd give up anything for you,
Even a hole or prison cell,
Would be paradise with you.

And I try, my love, to cage love,
To keep the storm at bay,
But it rages, love, inside or out,
It's wild and reckless and strong.

Meetings and partings they must end,
Though their joys are strong,
They pale, my love, in the dark of night,
To lie in the arms of the dark night sky.

Bethany Davis

And all my stars and all moonlight,
Are weak and pointless without you,
I love to lay in your loving arms,
My dark and loving sky.

Hold me, love, in your heart,
If it can't be in your arms,
And I'll try for strength and try so hard,
To cage my raging storm,
And 'til the time we lie again,
In each other's raging arms,
I'll try to hold the storm at bay,
To not utter again these words.

And I'm sorry, love, if these words cause pain,
Or are hard for you to read,
I try so hard to self-contain,
And not let them get the best one of me,
And this rambling poem that lost its way,
I will now bring to an end,
For the words could flow on endlessly,
If I didn't cage them up.

I love you, love, I love you so,
And I miss you oh so much,
But I close this here now on the ground,
Just know I love you so very much.

~September 19, 2018

The Gentle Speed of Breath

Your voice it soothes my wayward soul,
And calls my gypsy blood,
Like a waterfall in a hidden glade,
Or warm sun on a winter day,
I listen to each word you speak,
And every breath you take,
The sound of you that comes to me,
At the gentle speed of breath.

Your voice is like a salve to me,
That soothes all of my cares,
And forms a place for me to rest,
As in your arms to lay,
I love to hear your words or breath,
Or sigh that's barely heard,
The sound of you that comes to me,
At the gentle speed of breath.

A sigh that come before we part,
Or when our eyes do meet,
A whispered breath in the growing dark,
As you rest quietly asleep,
A word you speak that's full of love.
As you watch me from afar,
The sound of you that comes to me,
At the gentle speed of breath.

Your voice it soothes my wayward soul,
And calls my gypsy blood,
Like a waterfall in a hidden glade,
Or warm sun on a winter day,
I listen to each word you speak,
And every breath you take,
The sound of you that comes to me,
At the gentle speed of breath.

~October 12, 2018

Bethany Davis

There is My Only Home

I go to you whom I love so strong,
And have missed you oh so much,
The time that passed seems so long,
It's like it's been a full year and day,
But now I come and travel north,
To touch you once again,
To feel your arms around me tight,
There in my only home.

I go to you whom I missed so much,
To be with you finally once again,
Flying north with a smile wide,
To be with you once again,
In early winter's hazy cold,
And wind and chill and frost,
To share our warmth there skin on skin,
There in my only home.

I go to you whom I crave so bad,
With my soul and flesh and mind,
Touch on touch and skin on skin,
It's hard to be so very far apart,
Hand on breast and hip and thigh,
In passions strong raging flame,
Feeling lips and moving finger tips,
There in my only home.

~November 8, 2018

Bethany Davis

Our Lives Entwined

The journey was so long, my love,
To now from when we met,
Across the chasm that kept us apart,
And so many myriad things,
But now we're here in one place,
And have our lives entwined,
To live our days as we choose,
And each within arms' reach.

I love, my love, to lay awake,
Or lay in dreaming sleep,
With your arms around me tight,
Or your sleeping form so near,
Skin on skin to touch and kiss,
The thrill that never ends,
My kiss upon your naked back,
Or yours upon my neck.

Your hands my love that ever roam,
And touch my waiting skin,
A gentle touch upon my leg,
Or a kiss upon my breast,
A brush across my waiting hip,
Or your mouth upon my flesh,
The quiver passing from head to toe,
My lover's touch upon my skin.

Bethany Davis

It's amazing, love, to finally start,
And have the life we want,
To hold each other, kiss or touch,
Within each other's arms,
The passion strong that rages on,
Or the calm of a loving touch,
Whatever moves us at any time,
Instead of only when we can.

The journey was so long, my love,
To now from when we met,
Across the chasm that kept us apart,
And so many myriad things,
But now we're here in one place,
And have our lives entwined,
To live our days as we choose,
And each within arms' reach.

~April 15, 2019

Consider the Vastness

Consider the vastness,
Come with me, up, up,
Come up to the desolate places,
Up in the high mountains of Colorado,
Up where there are no higher mountains,
None higher than the range you stand on,
None higher for thousands of miles,
Up more than two miles above sea level,
Up there, in the heights,
Above the cities,
Above the towns,
Above the farms and ranches,
Up there, high up,
Beyond the tree line,
Up where life is small, careful,
Where most things can be crushed with a step,
Up where you are a giant to what is near,
But you are oh so small compared to what is before you,
Consider the vastness,
The whole world spreads out,
Spreads out before your feet,
Extending in a vast disk around,
Like a flat earth beneath a domed blue sky,
Consider the vastness,
The world stretching oh so far,
Consider that you are no bigger than the moss beneath your feet,
No bigger than the white and yellow flowers,
And mountain beneath your feet one with all the earth,
Consider the vastness,
And consider the earth,
One speck around one star,
One prick of light,

Bethany Davis

Wait,
As the sun sets,
As darkness rises and fills the sky,
As night spreads her wings,
Wait, as the stars appear,
One by one,
One by one,
Wait,
And consider,
Standing,
In a place far above the lights of the city,
In a place far above the lights of the smallest towns,
In a place far above the lights of houses and ranches,
Standing,
In a place so far and remote,
Alone in the desolate places,
Look up,
Look up,
Look up,
Consider the vastness,
Consider the expanse stretching before you,
The earth,
One speck,
The sun,
One star,
And consider what you see,
Stars on top of stars,
More stars than the mind can understand,
More stars than you've ever seen,
The Milky Way,
Stretching like a roaring river,
Like white paint,
But,
If you look closely,
Each star,
Distinct,
Defined,
A thousand specks of light,
A thousand thousand,
More thousands than the mind can know,

The Night's Sweet Embrace

Consider the vastness,
Look through the eyes of all there is,
Through the eyes of that vastness,
Gaze through the window of the soul,
Into the soul of the very fabric of all,
Consider the vastness,
Each star,
All those stars,
They are me,
My soul stretching inward like that canvas stretches up,
Consider the vastness,
Consider all those stars,
But consider the space between,
Consider the darkness,
The darkness,
That dark matter none can know,
That darkness holds each star,
Holds all the stars,
On and on the stars stretch,
And the darkness,
The night,
Holding each star,
Consider the vastness,
Consider that vastness,
And consider,
Out at the perimeter, there are no stars,
Where the light ends,
Where that vast sea of stars reaches its far shore,
Out where the outer darkness stretches,
The darkness continues,
The night has no end,
Out there,
Consider the vastness,
I consider the vastness,
Those stars,
Every star,
It is me,
They are me,
That sea of stars,
It is me,

Bethany Davis

Seeing myself,
Seeing myself reflected in the dark mirror,
The dark mirror that is her soul,
I see my beauty,
My majesty,
My vastness,
Because I see her see,
And in her darkness,
So vast I cannot reach its end,
In her darkness,
I am held,
Like all those stars,
In the silence of her shadowed wings,
And I consider,
I consider the darkness,
And I rest safe and secure,
Held in night's sweet embrace,
For I am her moon and stars,
And she is my dark night sky.

~May 4, 2017

ABOUT THE AUTHOR

Bethany Davis currently resides in Colorado with her true love. After many partings and meetings, that journey is done, and her Sophia has moved here from Saskatchewan. She currently works in an operations role for a technology company. She is the proud mother of a fey creature in the form of a cat, adopted mother of a bird in the form of a cat, is a part time vegan and part time meat connoisseur, and a walker of edges. Her life pursuit is to find beauty in all things. Bethany has been writing poetry and prose most of her life, among other pursuits.